Photo by Dan McNeil

A scene from the Denver Center Theatre Company production of "The Quick-Change Room." Set design by Michael Ganio.

THE QUICK-CHANGE ROOM

Scenes From A Revolution

BY NAGLE JACKSON

★

★

DRAMATISTS
PLAY SERVICE
INC.

2

THE QUICK-CHANGE ROOM, Scenes From a Revolution was produced by Denver Center Theatre Company (Donovan Marley, Artistic Director) in Denver, Colorado, on January 13, 1995. It was directed by Paul Weidner; the set design was by Michael Ganio; the costume design was by David Kay Mickelsen; lighting design was by Charles R. MacLeod; the original music was by Robert Sprayberry; the sound design was by Don Tindall; and the stage manager was Erock. The cast was as follows:

NINA	Erin J. O'Brien
MARYA	Peggy Pope
SERGEY	Tony Church
LENA	Alice White
NIKOLAI	John Hutton
LUDMILLA	Annie Murray
SASHA	Stephen Turner
BORIS	Alex Wipf
TIMOFEY	MichaelJohn McGann
ANNA	Jacqueline Antaramian

THE QUICK-CHANGE ROOM was developed in US WEST TheaterFest, in Denver, Colorado, in April, 1994. It was directed by Nagle Jackson. The cast was as follows:

NINA	Amy Prosser
MARYA	Kay Doubleday
SERGEY	Tony Church
LENA	Robynn Rodriguez
NIKOLAI	Frank Georgianna
LUDMILLA	Pamela Nyberg
SASHA	Nick Stabile
BORIS	Jamie Horton
TIMOFEY	Matthew Nowosielski
ANNA	Katherine Heasley

CHARACTERS

NINA — an actress in her twenties.

MARYA STEPANOVA — her mother.

LENA — (pronounced "LYENA") Marya's assistant, late forties.

SERGEY SERGEYEVICH TARPIN — Director of the Kuzlov Theater.

TIMOFEY — Sergey's assistant.

NIKOLAI — actor, middle aged.

LUDMILLA NEVCHENKA — prima donna actress, "of a certain age" ...

ANNA — a leading actress with the company, thirties.

BORIS — box office manager and Procurer.

SASHA — stage electrician.

PLACE

The Kuzlov Theater, St. Petersburg, Russia.

TIME

1991–1992

NOTE: Music for *The Moscow Express* has been composed by Robert Sprayberry and is available on request.

The main playing area is the Quick-Change Room itself, a mini-box set on a rolling platform that may move up and down stage, and which can be curtained off. When it is in the upstage position, the main stage area becomes the Rehearsal Room. There are two side stage areas: Sergey's Office stage right and a neutral area stage left.

THE QUICK-CHANGE ROOM

ACT ONE

Scene 1

In the Quick-Change Room.

Nina, a young woman in her 20s is standing in the center of the room talking to her mother, Marya Stepanovna.

NINA.   I am going to play Irina! I am going to play Irina in *The Three Sisters*. Oh, Mama ... Sergey Sergeyevich Tarpin sent for me to come to his office. To his *office*, Mama! A green carpet, very thick, and such furniture ... old Petersburg things. Posters all around. From the tour to Japan, the tour to Spain. A big poster from the U.S.A. of *Uncle Vanya*. And photos! There's a picture of him with Olivier in London, with Barrault in Paris.... What a life he has lived, Mama. *(Marya gestures: "Get on with it!")*

"Sit down, my dear Nina." He took off his glasses and said that. I sat down. He said: "I have watched your progress ever since you were a student at the Conservatory. I remember your work on Sonya. I remember your Juliet. There is a reason you were given a position here after only one year in the provinces." He stopped.

"Thank you, Sergey Sergeyevich," I said, and my voice sounded like a mouse or a kitten and I suddenly wanted to be home in my bed, all curled up and alone. But I was in the office of the Artistic Director and it was time to grow up. "If my work has been helpful to the Company, it is because of the excellent training I received — we all received — from you at the Conservatory, Sergey Sergeyevich." My breath control was magnificent. I said all of that in one breath, evenly, and using my lower register. The one Sasha says makes me sound like I've been up all night making love and drinking vodka, but I think it is probably, *actually*, the real me.

Anyway, Sergey Sergeyevich smiled and said: "We have marked you down for Irina in *The Three Sisters*. We shall begin rehearsals in two weeks and present our production sometime this fall. When we are ready." I said ... nothing. My eyes filled with tears. I'm sure I turned red as a flag.... "You are pleased?," he asked. "Oh, yes, Sergey Sergeyevich. I am as pleased as I have ever been about anything!" "Good," he said. "Learn the role. I don't want any actors standing around with books in their hands." "Sergey Sergeyevich," I said, "I *know* the role." "Good," he said. "Go take a nap." But I came here first, Mama, to tell you! *(Pause.)*

MARYA. Did he say anything about me? *(Blackout.)*

Scene 2

Stage left.

Sergey Sergeyevich Tarpin is addressing the Company, though we do not see them. Sergey is in his sixties, has dark, Georgian features and is dressed in suit and tie. He wears dark horn-rimmed glasses and always has a cigarette.

SERGEY. ... And so, my comrades, some will say, of course, "Why *The Three Sisters*? As members of this theater company, you have the right to ask ... why now? Why, when the great fundamental questions of the Socialist state are being debated, openly, and for the first time? Why in the warm spring of Comrade Gorbachev should we present a story of despair, of individual frustration and sloth?" Because: I see in the Prozorov family and in their associates, the same kind of fear so many of us are experiencing ... afraid to leave the old ways, ... afraid to "go to Moscow," just like the Sisters. In the sunlight of glasnost ... we are afraid of our own shadows. But this theater, founded by the Revolution and named for its beloved poet, is the theater of the *living*. And I, as your Artistic Director, will see that it remains so. We must find the melody and rhythm of Art which, like a good song, will help the Soviet people along their hard road to Communism!

Now about the soap: ... I am aware that the dressing rooms and lounges have been without soap. Dear Boris, the company Procurer, has been ... making arrangements with a ... supplier in Finland and we hope to have soap, at least by this winter. In the meantime ... *(He smiles.)* We shall simply have to love each other very much! Thank you. *(Blackout. Lights cross to:)*

Scene 3

The Quick-Change Room, as before.

MARYA. Did he say anything about me?

NINA. Well, no Mama. Why would he?

MARYA. You're my daughter. I thought we were all one big family here at the Kuzlov, but he says nothing about me?

NINA. Mama, there are two hundred employees of this theater —

MARYA. But *I'm* the Quick-Change Supervisor. Best in the business! I got Boris Godunov in coronation robes in twenty seconds flat, and they can't even do that at the Kirov! I'm *famous!* But now, I suppose, I'll just be somebody's *mother.* *(Timofey appears at the door, stopwatch in hand.)*

TIMOFEY. On your toes, ladies. Hop, hop, hop.... Nina, didn't Sergey tell you to take a nap?

NINA. Yes, Timofey.

TIMOFEY. Take a nap. *(He exits. An electric warning bell is heard. Lena enters.)*

LENA. Here we go.

NINA. *(Hugging.)* Lena! *Darling* Lena! I have such news!

LENA. I heard already. It's all over the Company. I'm so

happy for you, Ninchka!

MARYA. *(To Nina.)* Go, go. We've got a show to do. Give me a kiss ... *(Nina does.)* ... and go!

NINA. I'm gone! *(And she is.)*

MARYA. You got the headdress?

LENA. Yeah.

MARYA. Wig off, jacket on, robe on, hat on, beard —

LENA. — and the pipe in his mouth —

MARYA. Is it lit? *(Lena lights an elegant wooden pipe and takes a few puffs to get it going.)*

LENA. Good tobacco for a change. From Cuba maybe. *(Nikolai, a handsome, middle-aged actor, bursts into room.)*

NIKOLAI. Now! *(He stands with his arms raised. Marya pulls down his trousers and he steps out of them. She produces another pair which he steps into. Meanwhile, Lena slaps two gaudy, golden epaulets onto the shoulders of his jacket. She puts a military hat on his head. Marya pulls up and fastens his trousers. Lena puts the pipe in his mouth as Marya attaches his sword belt. It is all done in thirty seconds.)* The things I have to put up with! All that bitch has to do is come onstage and say: "So, Baron, I hear there is snow in the Caucasus." That's all she has to say: "snow in the Caucasus." So tonight she comes on ... hair to the *rafters* ... and she says to me: "So, Baron, I hear that winter has come, the rose petals have fallen, and the peasants are dropping like mayflies in the mountains of my youth." And I said to her: "Well, I don't know about any of *that*, you verbose and annoying princess, but I *have* heard there is snow in the bloody Caucasus!" Unbelievable! *(He races out.)*

MARYA. Good. We can relax.

LENA. "The Bloodsucker."

MARYA. Oh, Jesus, "The Bloodsucker." I put her clean out of my head. *(Reading change chart.)* "Change over-dress, add hat...." Look what she's done to it!

LENA. Seven years this show's in the repertory.

MARYA. And will be forever. Sergey loves it.

LENA. Boris says when the ruble is devalued and ticket prices go up, ... phhhft!

MARYA. Nonsense. People will always come to the theater.

8

In thirty years there's never been an empty seat. They may stop exploring space, they may stop having wars, but they'll never stop drinking vodka, having sex or going to the theater.

LENA. I hope so. *(Ludmilla Nevchenka enters to be changed. She is a Juno-esque actress, every inch the grande dame.)*

LUDMILLA. So. That man. All he has to say is: "Yes, there is snow in the Caucasus." *(Marya removes a copious skirt, circa 1870s, and we see Ludmilla's legs and heavy-knit Soviet underwear, beneath a bolster.)*

MARYA. You really should wear an underskirt, Ludmilla.

LUDMILLA. In that heat? I am in a spotlight all night. *(Marya puts a new skirt over the bolster as Lena puts on the jacket. To Marya.)* So, your little Nina will play Irina?

MARYA. What I hear.

LUDMILLA. Extraordinary. Someone must have bowed out.

MARYA. And you will be Olga?

LUDMILLA. *(Grudgingly.)* Uh-huh.

MARYA. *(To Lena, but for Ludmilla's benefit.)* That's the oldest sister.

LUDMILLA. Of course, I could have played Masha, but Anna wants it so, poor dear. And Sergey mentioned Natasha but I said "No." I don't play crude people. Vulgar people. But what they know about casting in this theater. I tell you. Ouch! You're pulling too tight! And careful with those stockings, Lenushka. Two days on line for those.

LENA. You stood two days — ?

LUDMILLA. I? When do I have time for things like that? My mother stood on line. Where's the mirror? *(She checks herself.)* So, the Wardrobe Mistress' daughter becomes the ingenue.... Things are changing in this country.... Off we go, then. *(She turns to leave, and as she does, we see that Marya has purposely left a wide gap open in the back of Ludmilla's skirt, revealing her legs and underwear. She exits.)*

LENA. Marya!

MARYA. She deserves it.

LENA. You'll hear about it. The Bloodsucker won't let that go unreported.

MARYA. An accident. Let's sit. *(They do.)* So, have you heard about a room?

LENA. My Katya says her friend at the Institute wants to stay until December. But then, maybe ... just imagine: a room of my own, and Katya could have our room all to herself.... Paradise!

MARYA. If they start giving Nina big parts ... who knows?

LENA. You'll get an apartment. I know you will! *(Sasha, a young man in overalls, enters.)*

SASHA. Where is she?

MARYA. Sasha!

SASHA. I want to congratulate her. I just heard.

MARYA. Look in the Artists' Lounge. She hangs around with that crowd now, Sasha.

SASHA. I'm not allowed in the Artists' Lounge. In our great classless society, electricians are not allowed there. I'm relegated to the Billiard Room upstairs.

MARYA. What do you care? You make the same money they do.

SASHA. It's always money with you, Marya.

MARYA. Yes, well.

SASHA. Things will improve.

LENA. They say the price of bread will double next month.

MARYA. Mother of God! Well, that'll be the end of Gorbachev!

SASHA. No. They like him in the West.

MARYA. Good. He can be mayor of New York.

SASHA. Still, it's our duty —

MARYA. Sasha, I think you are the only card-carrying Party member left in this organization. Who admits it, I mean.

SASHA. What about you? You're a Party member.

MARYA. Sashenka, my darling, the party's over. *(Nikolai enters in a rush.)*

NIKOLAI. So. *(They now do the reverse of the original quick change: restoring him to his first costume.)* Beard on, beard off ... I'm sick of this stupid play. *(To Sasha.)* Who are you?

SASHA. Plakoff. Sasha. Electrician.

NIKOLAI. Oh. New to the company?

SASHA. Seven years.

NIKOLAI. Ah. How do you do?

SASHA. How do you do ... *comrade. (The change is completed. Nikolai exits.)* For him I don't exist. And very soon, for Nina ...

MARYA. Nina loves you.

LENA. *(Smiling.)* Ahh ...

MARYA. What's wrong?

LENA. Oh ... love, you know ... I mean ... love. That's all. *(Sound: from offstage, roars of audience laughter. Ludmilla appears at the doorway in a rage.)*

LUDMILLA. You will pay for this, Marya Stepanovna! You will hear from the Committee of Artists!! *(Blackout. Lights up L.)*

Scene 4

Boris on the telephone.

Boris is a large bear of a man. He always wears a scarf.

BORIS. ... I am aware of that, Fyodor ... I am aware of that, too, Fyodor.... There is almost nothing I am not aware of, Fyodor.... Still, I need soap.... We are becoming known as the most highly gifted, highly paid and highly aromatic company in Leningrad.... Petersburg, then.... What's in a name, Fyodor?... I told you: I will give you the case of windshield wipers, *rubber* windshield wipers, I will give you the Turkish rug and I will set you up with Tatyana Borzhinski ... redhead ... from Warsaw ... I *thought* you'd be interested ... and three issues of *Hustler* ... deal?... Deal! *(He hangs up. Sasha enters holding a stage light.)*

SASHA. We have to get rid of these old things!

BORIS. What?

SASHA. Look at this spotlight, Boris. It was made in Hungary. *Before* the war! Unbelievable. It damn near electrocuted me just now.

BORIS. Why do you bother me with these things? I am in charge of the Box Office.

11

SASHA. Everyone knows you're the one who gets things. And when I go to Dubronin he just throws up his hands and says: "Inflation is at sixty percent. Inflation is at sixty percent!"

BORIS. Sasha, there is something I have to tell you.

SASHA. What?

BORIS. Inflation is at sixty percent. *(Blackout.)*

Scene 5

Sergey's office.

Ludmilla, in rehearsal clothes, is talking with Sergey.

LUDMILLA. *Mais non, mais non.* I think it's charming, Sergey. Really charming. And I'm sure with ... a lot of extra work ... she'll do splendidly. It is just that she is so very ... young. I am to be her sister ... well, you understand.

SERGEY. But Ludmilla, *ma chere,* you worry too much about these things. It is ... credible, certainly. It is certainly credible that you could be little Nina's older sister. And then, Chekhov never specifies how many years there are between the two ... as I recall, so —

LUDMILLA. So, It *does* look abnormal!

SERGEY. No, no, no. Not abnormal.

LUDMILLA. Unusual.

SERGEY. Not unusual. Not unusual. *(Timofey, Sergey's assistant, enters holding the same lighting instrument Sasha had. Timofey is a little martinet, neat and prim as a head waiter.)*

TIMOFEY. We have to get rid of these old things! *(Ludmilla slowly turns to him.)*

LUDMILLA. I beg your pardon?

TIMOFEY. Look, Sergey Sergeyevich: look at this lighting instrument. It was made in Hungary. *Before* the war! Unbelievable. But where is the money to replace it? Poor Sasha was nearly electrocuted.

SERGEY. But why do you bother me with these things?

TIMOFEY.   Because Dubronin just throws up his hands and says: "Inflation is at sixty percent! Inflation is at sixty percent!"

SERGEY.   It is true, my angel. Look at that, Ludi. That light has been in the theater longer than we have.

TIMOFEY.   We need an expression of authority, Sergey. You can do that.

SERGEY.   Maybe we should go back to candlelight.

LUDMILLA.   Well, it is true we use far too much light.

TIMOFEY.   That is what people want today. They want to see the truth. *(To Ludmilla, pointedly.)* Light *reveals*, does it not, Ludmilla?

LUDMILLA.   I have never cared for this little man. And I refuse to be insulted by ... mechanical persons. Au revoir, Sergey. *(She sweeps out.)*

SERGEY.   Not kind, Timofey. Distinctly not kind.

TIMOFEY.   Do you know ticket prices have gone up again?

SERGEY.   They have to, my angel.

TIMOFEY.   To thirty rubles!

SERGEY.   Thirty rubles!! Good God. No one will pay that much.

TIMOFEY.   Tonight will be the test. There's not been an empty seat in the Kuzlov Theater since 1919, except for during the Siege. Well. Now comes the *real* siege. And this time we may not survive. What the Nazis could not do, Perestroika may. *(Holds up instrument.)* And we need new lights! *(Blackout.)*

Scene 6

The Quick-Change Room.

Nina and Sasha are under the sheets of a little roll-away bed. They have just finished making love.

SASHA.   Did the first part feel good?

NINA.   Mmm, yes! And I loved it when you did that thing with ... your thing.

SASHA.   You mean the thing with your —

NINA.   When I put my leg over your —

SASHA.   — and that other thing was good, too ...

NINA.   Which?

SASHA.   When I got behind you, and you —

NINA.   You mean the thing with my hands?

SASHA.   Yeah, that was terrific, but also the thing where I got on my knees and —

NINA.   Was that after the first thing? I mean the thing with your thing underneath my —

SASHA.   No. That was later.

NINA.   Oh. *(Pause.)* Let's do it some more. *(Marya enters.)*

MARYA.   Give me all your rubles.

NINA.   What?! What are you doing here?

MARYA.   This is where I work.

NINA.   But you know Monday afternoons are our time to —

MARYA.   This is more important than sex. This is money. I'm taking all my money out of the bank and putting it in a private company. What they call a "corporation."

SASHA.   That's Capitalism!

MARYA.   Put your clothes on. Be a good boy, Sasha, and I'll let you in on the deal.

NINA.   *(To Sasha.)* You might as well.

SASHA.   What?

NINA.   Put your clothes on. *(He does, under the sheet.)* What company?

MARYA.   It's called "Moscow Nights, Incorporated."

SASHA.   Aha! Prostitution!

MARYA.   No. Pantyhose. They make pantyhose.

NINA.   If you put money in it can you *get* pantyhose?

MARYA.   Sure. Why not? They're gonna make pantyhose, real underwear, bras, even a line of fancy condoms.

SASHA.   *(Struggling with clothes.)* This is hopelessly corrupt!

MARYA.   You're getting out of my daughter's bed and you're calling underwear corrupt?

SASHA.   The State makes all those things. Those are necessities. People shouldn't be allowed to profit from necessities.

MARYA.   *(To Nina.)* Give me your rubles. The ones you keep in the tea can.

NINA.   No. I'm going shopping. For rehearsal clothes.

MARYA.   Oh my god, the *star*.

NINA.   I want something very feminine. Like Irina in the play.

SASHA.   Irina was a good Socialist. She wanted to work for the People. When we did *The Three Sisters* at the Komsomol Camp, I played Tusenbach.

MARYA.   And we all know what happens to him: bang-bang. Another idealist drops dead.

SASHA.   It's very tragic, I think.

MARYA.   Yeah, well … Chekhov always makes me laugh.

SASHA.   Laugh?! How can you *possibly* laugh at Chekhov?! He is —

NINA.   Go away, Sasha. I'm tired of hearing you and mother fight.

SASHA.   I'm going. But don't let her put your money in some decadent underwear company. Gangsters. That's what private collectives are. Mafia.

MARYA.   Good-bye, Sasha.

SASHA.   *(Kissing Nina.)* Good-bye, Ninchka. Capitalist or Socialist, I love you.

NINA.   Thank you, little bear. Bye-bye.

MARYA.   Good-bye, Sasha. *(He leaves.)* Poor fellow. He's on the wrong side of things.

NINA.   Do you think so?

MARYA.   Remember this, Nina: when systems change, learn how to use the system. That's how we made it through wars and czars and even Brezhnev. Every morning you get up you check the weather? Check the political climate, too. And that's the air you breathe.

NINA.   What if you don't agree with it?

MARYA.   You don't agree with air; you breathe it. *(Blackout. Timofey's voice is heard over P.A. system.)*

TIMOFEY.   *(Voice over P.A. system.)* There will be a meeting of the Artists' Committee at two o'clock this afternoon. In the Little Committee Room.

Scene 7

Committee Room.

Ludmilla seated, Sergey standing and speaking formally.

SERGEY.   In short, we cannot allow our revered artists, those actors and actresses who have given the great gift of their artistry to this company for so long — we cannot allow them to be insulted. Ludmilla Nevchenka asked me to bring this to the attention of the Artists Committee several weeks ago. Is there anything you would like me to add, Ludmilla my treasure? *(Sergey sits. Ludmilla stands.)*
LUDMILLA.   I would just like to say that I detect a pattern here. In these changing times, basic professional standards are being ignored. For a dresser to publicly insult a leading actress — or any actress — through a wanton act of mockery, — leaving me exposed that way for the entire audience to see my ... *back* — well, this is not the Kuzlov Theater that I have known. There was a time when Marya Stepanovna was a real worker, a true member of the Collective. But times have changed, and so has she, and she must be reprimanded and ... put in her proper place! That is why I have asked Sergey to bring this matter up before the Committee. Thank you, Sergey. *(She sits. Pause.)*
SERGEY.   It's a shame no one comes to these meetings anymore, Ludi. They used to be kind of fun ... *(Blackout.)*

Scene 8

The Quick-Change Room.

Boris talking to Lena.

BORIS.   — so I got the display cases for the lamb shanks.
LENA.   Why do we want to display lamb shanks?

BORIS. No, no. The display cases are for photos. Out front. We need photos out front.

LENA. You mean you *exchanged* the lamb shanks for the —

BORIS. I gave Gnady two pornographic films and a Billy Joel cassette for three dozen lamb shanks. Don't go to the Canteen today. Macaroni. Macaroni and water.

LENA. I can't afford the Canteen anymore, Boris. I eat bread and dried apples. Bread and dried apples, Boris! Is this what Lenin had in mind?

BORIS. *(Ignoring her.)* And now I have to bribe Maxie to take some photos. Something sensational. Last night we had a first for the Kuzlov Theater.

LENA. I heard.

BORIS. Twelve empty seats. But Sergey doesn't know. It'd kill him. And some people even left at intermission! The tickets cost a lot now, so suddenly they're all critics.

LENA. I heard, I heard.

BORIS. So we have to put something out front besides just a poster saying what's on. We gotta show Ludmilla with her tits sticking out. Tatyana's legs. Even Stiva's handsome mug. We'll get a shot of him as Hamlet. Shove some dishrags down his tights so it looks like he's really hung.

LENA. You don't need dishrags.

BORIS. What, bedsheets?

LENA. You don't need anything.

BORIS. He's hung?

LENA. Am I a dresser?

BORIS. Who'd've guessed. *(Marya enters.)*

MARYA. *(To Boris.)* Ah, Borya, you got my message. We need feathers.

BORIS. Get me those Nikes; I'll get you feathers.

MARYA. I asked Prokhov at the Corporation. He said he can get them, but not till February when his sister comes back from Tunisia.

BORIS. That's when you'll get the feathers. Shura has all kinds of feathers. Kilos of them. But he won't take anything except dollars or Nikes.

MARYA. Crook.

BORIS.   Businessman.

LENA.   Same thing. *(Nina enters. She is wearing a running out-fit, but it's cheap looking: colors too loud.)*

NINA.   Here comes the movie star after a hard day on the set!

MARYA.   God, I hope you didn't pay a lot for that.

LENA.   Where'd you get it, at the Universal?

BORIS.   *(Laughing.)* Looks like it. Looks like "Made in Ru-mania" to me!

NINA.   *(Crushed.)* Thank you very much … *(She sits.)* Just try-ing for something … fun. I can't afford very much, you know.

BORIS.   We can do better than that for you.

NINA.   *(Defensive.)* I *like* this.

BORIS.   You're going to be a leading lady now, Ninotchka … *(He sits next to her.)* Don't you worry. We'll take care of you. *(Blackout.)*

Scene 9

Sergey's Office.

Sergey is talking with Anna. Anna, in her young thirties and very pretty, has a 'chummy' sort of relationship with Sergey.

ANNA.   It is unbelievable, that's all.

SERGEY.   There are two kinds of belief, Anna: the belief of photographic naturalism and the belief of theatrical realism. We believe the fourth wall exists. We believe the painted back-drop is the skyline of Paris —

ANNA.   — We do *not* believe Ludmilla Nevchenka is Nina's big sister. Her big mother maybe. Her great aunt. Her old nanny —

SERGEY.   Don't exaggerate, my cherub.

ANNA.   Exaggerate?! *You* exaggerate. In the wrong direction. You exaggerate the audience's acceptance. Audiences won't accept what they're told to accept anymore. They accept and they believe what they *see*. Like in the West.

SERGEY.   The West, The West! You actors idolize the West and you've scarcely ever been there. I've been there. They only believe what they see, *but* what they see are all lies. That is what advertising *means*. And now I begin to see billboards on the Nevsky Prospekt showing me a beautiful woman using some sort of soap, and I'm supposed to believe my wife can look like that? Really.

ANNA.   The soap is unavailable anyway, so forget it. Let's talk about *The Three Sisters*, please.

SERGEY.   Ludmilla plays Olga. End of discussion. Delightful weather we're having.

ANNA.   Seryushka, listen to your Anna. Listen to the woman who shared your bed that summer in Yalta —

SERGEY.   Oh please!

ANNA.   Well it's true. We had a wonderful, romantic and rather athletic Crimean affair, and then shook hands and said to hell with it. You went back to Helga; I went back to my cat. But intimacy has its privileges.

SERGEY.   That was seven years ago.

ANNA.   At which time Ludmilla was too old for Masha, but you let her play the part anyway.

SERGEY.   If you must know, I promised her once ... long ago, that she would play all three of the Prozorov sisters. After her Irina in 1975.

ANNA.   She was too old for Irina in 1975; she was too old for Masha in 1983; and she's way too old for Olga now. She should play Anfisa.

SERGEY.   Anfisa is eighty.

ANNA.   Ludmilla can still get away with eighty.

SERGEY.   Now you're just being ridiculous.

ANNA.   *You're* the one who's —

SERGEY.   Look, the casting was accepted by the Workers' Committee —

ANNA.   They accept anything you tell them to.

SERGEY.   That is not true. *(Pause.)* That is no longer true. The Committee has developed alarming tendencies lately. Dissent for the sake of dissent.

ANNA. Well, who can blame them after all these years. Fresh air.

SERGEY. But artistic organizations are different from ... shoe factories. The Committee was there to be sure I'm not losing my grip, or cheating. I am not losing my grip; I have never cheated on anyone.

ANNA. Except your wife, except your wife, except your wife ...

SERGEY. Which would never have happened if I hadn't surprised her with that Bulgarian poet. Or if you hadn't been so damned attractive that particular summer ... but this is ancient history.

ANNA. *(Getting up.)* Well, I have tried, Sergey. I foresee nothing but trouble. You make the extraordinary gesture of elevating a very young girl to the status of principal actress, and then cast her as sister to an actress old enough to be her mother. And don't think Ludmilla isn't upset, as well. *(She kisses him on the cheek.)* And you'll hear about it. That I guarantee you, Seryushka. You'll hear about it! *(Lights crossfade to:)*

Scene 10

The Rehearsal Room.

Timofey is preparing the rehearsal. The three ladies are milling about. Nikolai enters.

TIMOFEY. Please, please. For the first scene. Just the sisters. Ludmilla darling. The window will be up here. *(She goes to it.)* That's right. Ninitchka, please. Seated there, yes. *(Nina sits in chair.)* And Anna on the chaise longue, of course, reading ... *(Anna drapes herself picturesquely.)* A lovely spring morning.... The three sisters at rest ...

NIKOLAI. Sergey is coming up the hall.

TIMOFEY. Enter: Sergey Sergeyevich! *(Sergey comes into the room, followed by Boris.)* They are ready, Sergey.

SERGEY. My friends, I have shocking news.

ANNA. Seryushka?

SERGEY. Tonight at the Kuzlov Theater ... for the first time since the reopening after The Great Patriotic War ... the house will be less than full.

LUDMILLA. How do you know? It's only one in the afternoon.

BORIS. We still have one hundred seats to sell. We won't sell that many by seven o'clock. Not for *Brothers in the Snow.*

LUDMILLA. We shouldn't be doing *Brothers in the Snow.*

SERGEY. I will decide repertory, thank you very much.

LUDMILLA. Maybe not.

ANNA. Ludi! Don't.

TIMOFEY. This is treason! This is ... individualism!

BORIS. This is box office. I know what Ludmilla means. The *public* may decide repertory.

NIKOLAI. But the public has always filled the house for *Brothers in the Snow* before. I happen to think they rather enjoy my performance as Andrey, if you want to know.

BORIS. The public came to *anything* because the theater is warm, the tickets were cheap and the theater cafe is the only place in Petersburg where you can get real ham and German cheese.

ANNA. Also coffee. I have an aunt who comes all the way from her place on the Vyborg Side just for the coffee. I ask her what she thought of the play, she says: "I had three cups and an ice cream."

SERGEY. Please, Anna.

ANNA. She sleeps through the play.

NIKOLAI. After all that coffee?

LUDMILLA. Must have been *Brothers in the Snow.*

SERGEY. Stop all this! I just wanted you to know that we must work very hard. Ticket prices have gone up. Even the cafe prices have gone up. We must produce an extraordinary *Three Sisters,* to win a new, ... somewhat more cosmopolitan and affluent audience.

TIMOFEY. *(Grumbling.)* Gangsters ... mafia ...

BORIS. People who invest wisely are not —

TIMOFEY. How would you know? You're one of them!

21

SERGEY. Timofey! Everyone! Silence!! *(Pause.)* Hello, Ninchka, my treasure. I'm sorry on your first day of rehearsal you must be subjected to this ugliness. All the old geese a-cackling, eh? But the beautiful young swan keeps her silence ... and glides ... *(He takes her hand and leads her into a dance twirl.)* ... like a princess over the water ...

NINA. *(Loving it.)* I am a bird.... I am a sea gull ...

LUDMILLA. Thank god we're not doing *that* play! *(Sergey is dancing with Nina.)*

SERGEY. Is this what the public wants, Boris? Movement ... and youth ... and beauty!

TIMOFEY. *(Applauding.)* Bravo, Sergey. Brava Ninchka.

LUDMILLA. *(Loudly.)* "Just a year ago father died. The fifth of May."

SERGEY. *(Getting down to business.)* Quite right, Ludi. Thank you. To work, to work. But you know, Ludmilla my flower, we mustn't *announce* it like that. Like a herald. Like the town crier.

LUDMILLA. You're comparing my acting to the town crier?

SERGEY. Ludi, no! Oh for heaven's sakes, if we cannot speak constructively, if we cannot make suggestions! *(He sits in his chair.)*

TIMOFEY. You are the director, Sergey! *(Pause. Sergey rises.)*

SERGEY. Now this is what I want, my three beautiful jewels: silence. A long moment of silence at the beginning. The silence of midday. "It is noon" writes Chekhov. "There is snow." I want ... I want to hear the snow ...

TIMOFEY. *(Writing.)* I shall tell the Sound Department.

SERGEY. *(To Timofey.)* There *is* no sound, you idiot! That is precisely what is so ... so beautiful ... so touching, and yet unreal. The curtain rises on absolute silence. We hear, we *hear* people thinking. *(Pause. A long silence. Boris tiptoes out. His shoes squeak.)* Oh!

BORIS. Sorry, Sergey.

SERGEY. Shhh!

TIMOFEY. Shhh!

SERGEY. Be quiet, Timofey.

TIMOFEY. Yes, Sergey. *(Boris is gone. Silence.)*

SERGEY. And then ...

LUDMILLA. *(Exactly as before.)* "Just a year ago —

ANNA. My god!

LUDMILLA. — father died. The fifth of May —"

ANNA. You scared me half to death!

SERGEY. Ludmilla, really! It is to *yourself.*

LUDMILLA. *(Very softly.)* "Just a year ago father died.... The fifth of May —

SERGEY. Even *less ...*

LUDMILLA. ... the *fourth* of May —"

SERGEY. Oh please!

LUDMILLA. "Your name-day, Irina."

SERGEY. But you must speak *to* Irina.

LUDMILLA. First you say "speak to yourself," then you say "speak to Irina." Really, Sergey, this is not like you.

SERGEY. Get on with it.

LUDMILLA. "It was snowing ... I could barely stand up ... and you ... *(She turns to Nina.)* ... you fainted dead away. You looked like a corpse" ... *(Nina smiles up at her.)* Well, of course, if she's going to grin at me like that!

SERGEY. What's wrong?

LUDMILLA. It's not very corpse-like, is it? And look at her: the picture of health. Robust. This is the delicate little flower who faints?

NINA. It was a year ago.

ANNA. She was not even twenty.

LUDMILLA. *(To Timofey, who is on book.)* Does it say that?

NINA. Yes. *(Pause.)*

LUDMILLA. *(To Nina.)* I beg your pardon? I believe I was addressing the regisseur.

NINA. Yes, but, excuse me Ludmilla, it's my line, you see. I say it to you, in fact: "I'm still a little girl to you," I say. "But in fact I'm already twenty."

ANNA. Extraordinary.

LUDMILLA. What is?

ANNA. That the Prozorovs — our parents — stretched out their childrearing over such a *long* period.

TIMOFEY. Olga is twenty-eight.

ANNA. Oooh my. Well, right there we've got a tiny problem, haven't we?

SERGEY. Anna —

ANNA. If Olga is twenty-eight, Masha must be at *best* twenty-six. And I am not twenty-six.

SERGEY. It will all look fine.

LUDMILLA. No. Anna is right. It will look absurd. Nina is simply too young. Let her play Natasha. She's a *perfect* Natasha.

TIMOFEY. Tatyana is playing Natasha.

LUDMILLA. Who is Tatyana?

ANNA. From Warsaw. Gorgeous. From Warsaw.

LUDMILLA. Who are all these new people? Poles? Why don't I even meet them?

NINA. *I* am playing Irina. *(Pause.)*

LUDMILLA. Fine. But I am not playing Olga.

SERGEY. Ludchka ... my kitten —

LUDMILLA. We'll let the Workers' Committee decide.

SERGEY. *(Livid.)* The Workers' Committee does not decide casting!

LUDMILLA. Well maybe they should!

TIMOFEY. This is counter-revolutionary ... this is —

ANNA. Shut up, Timofey.

SERGEY. Shut up, Timofey.

NINA. *(With a little tear.)* I'm sorry I've caused all this trouble ...

SERGEY. It's not *you*, my cherub.

LUDMILLA. Yes it is, Sergey. You are under the spell of that one.

ANNA. Ludmilla!

LUDMILLA. He always falls for the cadets, *"les jeunes filles du Conservatoire"!* His pretty little students who fawn over him. If you'd look at their talent instead of their ... petticoats! —

SERGEY. I refuse to listen to this rubbish. I am leaving. Timofey!

TIMOFEY. Yes, Sergey Sergeyevich!

LUDMILLA. — not to mention the entire question of *class*.

TIMOFEY. We live in a class-less society!

ANNA. Ha!

SERGEY. *(To Ludmilla.)* What are you implying?

LUDMILLA. We all know Nina's background. It's very ...

quaint.

SERGEY.   She comes from the *theater!* It is the finest background imaginable. Your own mother, Ludmilla, was a ballet dancer.

LUDMILLA.   Yes, but she didn't *dress* ballet dancers!

SERGEY.   Silence! I will not listen to bourgeois poison. The rehearsal is over!

TIMOFEY.   The rehearsal is over! *(Pause. A long silence.)*

SERGEY.   *(Beaming.)* There, you see? *That* is the kind of silence I'm looking for. *(Nina runs from the room in tears. Lights fade.)*

Scene 11

The Quick-Change Room.

Boris seated with notebook; Marya and Lena looking at him in disapproval.

BORIS.   I am only taking notes.

MARYA.   Notes? How can we work when you're sitting there staring at us?

BORIS.   Marya Stepanovna, as you know, we are going through difficult times. I have been asked to inspect each department to see if ... to be sure things are being done efficiently.

MARYA.   What could possibly be more efficient than a quick-change room ? That's what it's *for.*

LENA.   And Marya is the *best.* I worked at the Pushkin before I came here. They had *twelve* dressers in the quick-change room. Everyone got in everyone's way. My Katya worked there for a while —

BORIS.   She was let go.

LENA.   How did you know that?

BORIS.   I know everything, Lena. That is my job. *(Nina bursts in, in tears.)*

NINA. Mama! *(Marya rushes to her, hugs her.)*

MARYA. What's wrong? What is it?

LENA. *(Indicating Boris should leave.)* Borya …

BORIS. I'll just sit. *(He does.)*

NINA. That Ludmilla!

LENA. "The Bloodsucker."

MARYA. What, she's making difficulties? Of course she's making difficulties.

NINA. She's horrid to me. She doesn't want me in the play.

BORIS. She doesn't want you as Irina because it makes her look like your old nanny. She's right, too. It's absurd.

MARYA. Boris!

BORIS. I mean it. It's absurd for Ludmilla to be cast as Olga. No one wants to see her anymore, anyway. I can't sell tickets to see these old warhorses. Nina, darling, I want to have photos taken of you. For the front of the theater.

NINA. You … you do?

MARYA. *(Beaming.)* There, you see?!

BORIS. You are the future. You are the future of the Kuzlov Theater. *(An electric warning bell is heard.)*

LENA. Matinee beginning.

MARYA. We're ready. Cheer up, Ninchka. Boris is right. If it comes to a fight between Ludmilla and you, you'll win. It's a new Russia! *(Music heard. Nikolai enters.)*

NIKOLAI. Bring the armor. I need you in the wings.

LENA. Yes, yes …

MARYA. *(Gathering up costume.)* We're coming, we're coming. Don't be such a nervous old queen. *(Marya, Lena and Nikolai exit.)*

NINA. *(To Marya.)* Where's Sasha?

MARYA. *(From offstage.)* Who knows!

BORIS. You don't need Sasha, Nina my darling. Sasha is thirty years old, but fifty years behind the times.

NINA. Sasha has ideals.

BORIS. He was a Komsomol brat. He still behaves as if the Party were important.

NINA. It's not?

BORIS. They're going to outlaw the Party. Very soon. Gorby

has had it with them.

NINA.   Outlaw Communism?! It's what we were all striving for.

BORIS.   But nobody wanted. You must begin to think in a new way, Ninotchka. I am going to re-do this theater.

NINA.   You? You're the Box Office manager, the Procurer!

BORIS.   Only a matter of time, Nina. By the end of next summer ...

NINA.   What?

BORIS.   *(Smiling.)* Summer will end! *(He embraces her.)* My adorable Ninchka ...

NINA.   How is your wife, Boris?

BORIS.   She's fine, fine. *(He pulls away.)*

NINA.   And the boys?

BORIS.   Ah well, Fedya, you know ...

NINA.   What's wrong?

BORIS.   Very ill, Nina. Something in the blood. I can't get the medicine he needs, can't get the doctors. In the West, of course, they can do things ...

NINA.   Boris, you've got to take him.

BORIS.   Where does the money come from? And when I look at him lying there like that ... it makes me so goddamn *mad!....* *(He pounds his fist on the furniture. Music and applause are heard.)*

NINA.   You, of all people, should know how to get money.

BORIS.   Sometimes. I am learning. *(Marya and Lena enter.)*

MARYA.   Quick ... quick, get ready. Boris, you're in the way.

BORIS.   I'll be observing. Like a tiny bedbug. You will never notice.

MARYA.   *(To Lena.)* The minute he walks in: coat, trousers ... where is the hat?

NINA and LENA.   *(Simultaneously.)* Here.

MARYA.   You take notes on *this,* Boris. This is the quickest change of all. Almost. *(Sasha enters.)*

SASHA.   Nina! Everyone! Have you heard — *(Marya and Lena take off his trousers and slap a wig on his head. Sasha talks to Nina throughout this, too upset to notice.)* I would have come sooner, but I was in the Billiard Room. Petya came running in. "Turn on the radio," he said. And so we did and of course it didn't *work*, so then we all ran into the Prop Shop and there was Vera standing in the middle of the room and crying and — *(He notices for the first time that they've removed his trousers.)* What are you doing?!!

NINA.   Mama! It's Sasha!

MARYA.   Sasha! What the hell are you doing here? During a performance! Where's Nikolai? *(Nikolai enters throwing armor pieces on floor.)*

NIKOLAI.   Quick! Quick! Change me! *(They leave Sasha, costume trousers down, and give the same treatment to Nikolai, changing his trousers, but they put Sasha's pants on him instead.)*

SASHA.   *(To Nina and Boris.)* Have you heard? Gorbachev has been kidnapped!

NINA.   Kidnapped!

SASHA.   He's supposed to come back from his *dacha* in Georgia today. But he hasn't shown up.

NIKOLAI.   These are the wrong pants!!

MARYA.   Oh my god!

SASHA.   Those are my pants!

LENA.   *(To Sasha.)* Take off your pants!

SASHA.   *(Looking down.)* My god, these aren't mine!

NINA, LENA, MARYA and NIKOLAI.   OFF!! *(Sasha takes his pants off, exchanging them with Nikolai who's quick-change is now completed. Timofey enters.)*

TIMOFEY.   Nicky! You're on! *(Nikolai darts out.)* I thought this was a quick-change room! *(He exits.)*

MARYA.   *(To Sasha.)* You idiot! How dare you come in here during a performance?!

SASHA.   Comrade Gorbachev is through! There has been a coup!

LENA.   *(Beating her breast.)* Oh my god, oh my god ...

MARYA.   Who told you?

SASHA.   On the radio. And then the news stopped and they just played Tchaikovsky. You know what that means, when they play Tchaikovsky! *(Boris bolts from the room.)*

LENA.   Holy Mother of God ...

NINA.   What will happen to us now?

MARYA.   What always happens: we'll get shit on.

NINA.   Oh dear ... I wonder ...

SASHA.   What?

NINA.   I wonder if we'll cancel rehearsals ...

MARYA.   Lena, turn on the radio. *(Lena does:* The Symphonie Pathétique.*)*

MARYA and LENA.   Tchaikovsky. *(Lights fade to black.)*

Intermission

ACT TWO

Scene 1

Sergey addressing the Company.

Lights up stage left on Sergey.

SERGEY.   ... and so my comrades ... my *friends,* rather ... we must change with the times. What did Anton Pavlovich write in *The Cherry Orchard?* "A new kind of living is just around the corner. A happy one. And we are the ones creating it!" Yes, my fellow artists, an era of prosperity and comfort is very close now. Can you imagine it? No more endless lines, no more tiny apartments, sharing with god-knows-who ... and god-knows-why! But, of course, this demands from all of us ... a period of adjustment.... Accordingly, and in line with the changes being effected in our government, we will no longer offer any kind of recognition to the Communist Party.

I was, as you know, a loyal Party member for years, since before many of you were born. Well. That is over. The Party had become the very thing it was invented to replace: a stifling bureaucracy, a hotbed of personal privilege and opportunism.

So.

What this means of course ... is a change in some of our repertory. I am sorry to say that Lev Brudsky's sensitive tragedy, *Brothers in the Snow,* will be dropped from the repertory. As will *Forward We March,* and that charming comedy, *Pavlov's Daughter,* in which Ludmilla Nevchenka shone so radiantly.

A new financial reality has hit us now that ticket prices have quadrupled due to inflation. We must find ways to fill our seats. Our beautiful new production of *The Three Sisters* will be, I am confident, a tremendous hit, and ... we are currently rethinking it to conform to the more ... popular taste. I am also happy to announce that next season we will present a new spectacle which I am sure will take St. Petersburg by storm. It is a deeply artistic and romantic study of man's triumph over sickness and deformity. It is called ... *The Phantom of the Opera!* *(Crossfade to:)*

Scene 2

The Quick-Change Room.

Sasha holding a valise. Nina trying on costumes.

SASHA.   So what was it all about? After all? My grandparents survived the Siege of Leningrad. Baba still refuses to call it St. Petersburg. Leningrad was a great city of the War. Leningrad and Stalingrad. They would not fall. And now they've vanished from the lexicon.

NINA.   That's all history, Sasha. The whole thing was a fake, anyway.

SASHA.   Hitler was a fake?!

NINA.   No, but ... well, for instance the Siege. Boris told me that Stalin deliberately allowed that to happen because he hated Leningrad.

SASHA.   I'm not praising Stalin. God forbid. But you can't fault the dream. Even Boris, with his petty bourgeois opportunism, his ... his criminal survivor economics, cannot deny that the dream was a noble one: Socialism, eventually leading to a community of mankind. "From each according to his abilities, to each according to his need."

NINA.   Yeah, and what about *her* need?

SASHA.   It's a figure of speech, Nina.

NINA.   Women were treated like shit in the Party.

SASHA.   No!

NINA.   Yes! We were supposed to go and build railroads, teach school, gather the harvest — and *then* come home and

31

feed our husbands who were usually drunk. And clean the apartment, do the laundry, raise the brats —

SASHA. That was never the plan.

NINA. No. It was life. And it's the difference between the Plan and Life that finally destroyed the whole bloody thing, thank god.

SASHA. So now there is no dream?

NINA. That's right. Now there's reality. *(Displays costume.)* Isn't this pretty? Act one.

SASHA. My train leaves in an hour. From the Finland Station.

NINA. Your folks will be so happy to have you back home.

SASHA. Yes ... I didn't tell them I was laid off. I just said I had decided to move back there. Now that we can come and go without restrictions

NINA. You see? That's good, isn't it?

SASHA. Oh sure! We can come and go. And we can get laid off because no one can afford to pay their employees anymore. I had a lifetime contract, Nina. So do you. Well, that all went up in smoke, didn't it? "Free to come and go." Hah! Free to live in the street!

NINA. I'm sorry about the cutbacks, Sashenka. You know I am. But you could've found something right here in Peter, I'm sure.

SASHA. Naw, it's hopeless. And besides ... I don't like the atmosphere anymore. It's an ugly place now.

NINA. Petersburg will always be beautiful, Sasha.

SASHA. See if you think so when *your* contract is revoked. *(Boris enters.)*

BORIS. Ninchka ... ah, Sasha. You are leaving us.

SASHA. Try not to weep real tears, Boris.

BORIS. *(Holding out a bag.)* In fact, I have brought you something. This is for your parents. Instant coffee. You can't get it in the provinces. And only for hard currency here.

SASHA. Why would they want instant coffee?

BORIS. Well, if you don't want it —

NINA. It costs a fortune, Sasha!

SASHA. *(Taking the bag.)* Yes, well ... thank you, Boris. They can barter it for something.

BORIS. Of course.

SASHA. Where'd you steal it?

BORIS. Oh, our former Communist is a little bit spiteful, I think. Just a little bit ... naive, wouldn't you say, Nina?

NINA. Nevertheless ... I'll miss you, Sashenka. *(She goes to him.)* I'll miss your great lovely eyes ... and your scrubby cheek. And some other things as well.

SASHA. *(Embarrassed.)* Nina!

NINA. *(To Boris.)* Sasha is a wonderful lover.

BORIS. That's because he's got some gypsy blood. Like me. Gypsies are great lovers.

SASHA. I must go. You can't even come with me to the station?

NINA. Sasha ... you know I've got rehearsal.

SASHA. When will they open that damn thing? It's been months and months.

NINA. You know Sergey. He'll open when he wants to.

BORIS. He'll open when *I* want to. Sasha, my good fellow, give my love to the countryside. There's a lot of action out there for a smart boy like you. Believe me.

NINA. My god, you're really leaving, aren't you! *(Throws her arms around him.)* Really, really, really ... I won't have my adorable Sashenka to kiss.

SASHA. I know ... I know. I will miss you terribly!

NINA. You'll *write.*

SASHA. Yes, I'll write. Everything is changing ... everything happens so fast now. *(Marya enters.)*

MARYA. Sasha. Haven't you left yet?

NINA. Oh, Mama, he's leaving ... he's really *leaving.*

MARYA. All men leave; it is a rule of life. Your father left seven times before he really left.

BORIS. Where *is* Yuri?

MARYA. The Baltics, with the engineers. Now they're independent, I live in terror he'll come back.

SASHA. I must go.

MARYA. *(Holding out bag.)* Here, Sasha. For you. For your mother. Rose water. I made it myself.

33

SASHA. Beautiful ... beautiful. Thank you Marya Stepanovna. I have always had the highest respect for you.

MARYA. The perfect gentleman! I shall miss you. *(They hug.)* Now you go. You'll miss your train.

SASHA. Yes.... Good-bye, all ... Boris ... Nina ... Nina, at least walk with me to the Stage Door.

NINA. Yes. Of course.

SASHA. Good-bye, Quick-Change Room ... Good-bye, ... *Theater! (Nina and Sasha leave.)*

MARYA. Nina can do *much* better. But he was an honest person.

BORIS. I have bad news for you, Marya.

MARYA. Why should you be any different? Well?

BORIS. We will have to let Lena go.

MARYA. Ah, no. No! There I really must put my foot down. Absolutely not. No.

BORIS. I'm afraid it's a decision you have nothing to do with.

MARYA. I shall take this to the Grievance Committee.

BORIS. Those committees are all defunct now, Marya.

MARYA. You mean I have no recourse?

BORIS. You can leave.

MARYA. I have a contract for life with this Collective!

BORIS. So does everyone. Contracts are meaningless now.

MARYA. This is Perestroika?

BORIS. This is economic reality.

MARYA. I preferred the fiction! Everyone had jobs. Everyone ate. If that's "fiction," give me fairy tales! I can't get along without Lena. *(The electric warning bell is heard.)*

BORIS. You will have to.

MARYA. Who replaces her?

BORIS. No one.

MARYA. One person can't do this job. It takes four hands. At least. *(Lena enters, ready for work.)*

LENA. Here's Anna's hat. They've rung the first bell. Hello, Boris. *(Boris bows. He indicates "shh" to Marya.)*

MARYA. It's insane what you're doing.

BORIS. Enough now. *(Nikolai enters. He wears a three-corner hat.)*

NIKOLAI. Did you take my three-corner hat?

LENA. No. We don't have it.

NIKOLAI. It's not in my dressing room.

LENA. We don't have it, Niki. How many do you have in this show?

NIKOLAI. Just the one.

LENA. It's on your head.

NIKOLAI. What?... *(Feels it.)* Oh. *(Sits.)* I'm losing my mind. I'm losing my mind, Boris. They've let Gnady and Pierre go. I have to play Suslov *and* Sadovsky now! *(Bell rings.)* Oh my god ... *(Rises.)* ... What are we coming to? What is it all *coming* to?... *(He exits.)*

LENA. Poor man.

MARYA. It's crazy. It's crazy what you're doing, Boris.

LENA. I have to tell someone! My Katya's found a wonderful job! *And* we'll be moving to a new apartment. Two rooms and a kitchen, all to ourselves!

BORIS. How did she manage that?

LENA. She's been keeping it a secret. But finally I said to her: "Katya, these new clothes ... this perfume ... where does it come from?" And she told me: She's working. As a hostess. At the Evropeskaya Hotel. Showing tourists around and so on. But not Intourist; not KGB, I swear.

BORIS. How did she get a job like that? It must have cost a bundle.

LENA. Ah, my Katya. She's a clever girl.

BORIS. Well, that's nice, Lena. Now you're all set up. She can support you for a change.

LENA. I would never permit that. But together ... we'll do very well, I think. *(Music is heard.)*

MARYA. Are we ready for Anna?

LENA. Hat.

MARYA. Check.

LENA. Cloak.

MARYA. Yes. And gloves.

LENA. Wait a minute ... they're in the box. *(Nina enters.)*

NINA. Well, he's gone. I can't believe it. Sasha is gone.

BORIS. Life changes.

LENA. "Change is good," Katya always says.

BORIS. Well, there you are then. *(Anna enters for change.)*

ANNA. Hello, ladies. Boris!

BORIS. I shall leave. *(They change Anna as Nina takes Boris D.)*

NINA. Boris, you know Sergey keeps talking about Irina, about ... the music of her soul. The way she moves and so on. And I wonder ... don't you think that's what we need in this production?

BORIS. What do you mean?

NINA. Music.

BORIS. There'll be music, of course.

NINA. No, I mean *really*. I mean singing.

BORIS. You want to sing?

NINA. Yes!

BORIS. Ask Sergey, not me.

NINA. Lately whenever I ask him anything he says: "Can't afford it. Ask Boris."

BORIS. Yes, life is easy for him now; he's got someone else to blame. *(Anna's change is completed.)*

MARYA. There you are.

ANNA. Thanks. *(She exits.)*

MARYA. Nina, your dress is over there. I re-did the cuffs.

NINA. Thank you, Mama. *(She goes behind dressing screen to try on the dress. Nikolai enters.)*

NIKOLAI. So. *(Marya and Lena change him from a dandy to a monk, as:)*

MARYA. You see, Boris? You see how it goes?

BORIS. Just a question of readjustment.

LENA. That's what my Katya says. I say: "Really, Katushka, we can't afford this new place." "Yes we can," she says!

NIKOLAI. Hat.... *Hat!*

MARYA. Yes, yes. Here.

LENA. "Yes," she says, "we must readjust our values." We must readjust our *rubles*, I say!

NIKOLAI. Thank you, ladies. *(He exits.)*

LENA. It's all like a dream come true.

NINA. *(From behind dressing screen.)* What is?

LENA. We're moving. To a real apartment. Just for us!

NINA. How can you afford it?

LENA. Katya has a new, wonderful job. And that, with my salary here, will just work out. You see? *Patience,* as I've always said.

MARYA. *(Glaring at Boris.)* Yes. Isn't it wonderful!

BORIS. I must go. *(Nina comes from behind screen wearing only a camisole.)*

NINA. Boris?

MARYA. Nina, cover yourself. *(Throws her a robe which Nina clutches to herself.)*

BORIS. Yes?

NINA. Remember: *music.*

BORIS. *(Pointing to Nina.)* That's it!

MARYA and NINA. What?

BORIS. That's the pose I need for the poster out front. Nina, in her ... whatever that is ... clutching her little dress ... "Irina Dressing For The Ball."

MARYA. Nina? Like that? In front of the theater?!

LENA. "Irina Dressing For The Ball".... There's no ball in *The Three Sisters.*

BORIS. But with music ...

NINA. *(Dropping robe.)* Yes, Boris!

BORIS. Maybe there *will* be! *(Nina runs to embrace him.)*

MARYA. Lena?

LENA. Yes?

MARYA. He's firing you. He's letting you go. *(Blackout.)*

Scene 3

Timofey addressing the Company.

TIMOFEY. Here are the new rules of protocol as regards nomenclature, privilege of facility, access to gratuities, etc. "The Grand People's Theater Collective and Conservatory of Leningrad Named in Honor of V. Kuzlov," the G.P.T. as we call it, will no longer be known as such. "The Grand People's

Theater Collective and Conservatory of Leningrad Named in Honor of V. Kuzlov" will henceforward be known as the "The Grand People's Theater Collective and Conservatory of Saint Petersburg," period. Sergey Sergeyevitch Tarpin, our esteemed and beloved Producing Artistic Director, will no longer be known as Producing Artistic Director. He will henceforward be known as Resident Director. I myself, Timofey Vassilyevitch Bubnov, will no longer be referred to as Assistant to the Producing Artistic Director and Regisseur, but as Administrative Aide. It is also to be noted that our esteemed Boris, hitherto referred to as Manager of Box Office Control, will now be known as Exclusive Director of Marketing, Publicity and Repertoire. Because of these added obligations he will be leaving his Box Office cubicle and will occupy an office ... on the second floor. *(Crossfade to:)*

Scene 4

The Rehearsal Room.

Anna, Ludmilla and Sergey are examining the chaise longue.

ANNA. Can it be fixed?

LUDMILLA. Of course it can. I've got a needle and thread in my bag.

SERGEY. What a shame. All these old things ...

ANNA. Remember when Trofimov fell off this in the seduction scene in ... what was it?

SERGEY. *(Laughing.) The Death of Tarelkin.*

ANNA. Yes!

LUDMILLA. Don't remind me; I was the maid!

ANNA. He was so humiliated, he just stayed there. On the floor! *(All three are laughing now. Old home week.)*

SERGEY. We used this in *Hedda Gabler,* too.

LUDMILLA. Oh ... don't remind me. Such joy ... such a time of joy ...

ANNA.   You were a wonderful Hedda.

LUDMILLA.   And your Thea! ... so vibrant, so —

ANNA.   *(Smiling.)* "Young," you were going to say.

SERGEY.   It wasn't so long ago.

LUDMILLA.   It was twelve years ago, Sergey. During what we are now told was the Time of Stagnation. Well.

SERGEY.   We could do no wrong in those days.

ANNA.   *Enemies, Cyrano, Equus* ... and the Pirandello plays. We were ...

LUDMILLA.   Magnificent.

SERGEY.   We were ... very good.

LUDMILLA.   *Magnificent. (To Sergey.) You* were magnificent. And the tours: Japan, Argentina, London and Madrid —

SERGEY.   Truth to tell, Ludi, they didn't much like us in London.

LUDMILLA.   London is nothing but gay boys and American musicals. Who cares about London?

ANNA.   It was the wrong theater. That big old barn. We were lost up there making our strange Slavic noises no one could understand. They looked at us as if we were Eskimos. And we were politically very unpopular at that time. *Now* if we were to tour!

SERGEY.   Now there's no money. We are politically above reproach and poor as beggars.

LUDMILLA.   Well, that's what they like, isn't it? To see us grovel? Yes?

ANNA.   Can we fix the furniture, please?

LUDMILLA.   You hold the edges together ... it's a shame such fine old upholstery just rots away like this ... *(She kneels on floor beside chaise to repair it.)*

ANNA.   Well, we sit on it, lie on it, jump on it ...

SERGEY.   Fuck on it.

LUDMILLA.   Sergey!

SERGEY.   It's true! Timofey found Yuri and one of the little seamstresses in here, huffing and puffing. "Stop! Stop!!," said Timofey. "That furniture belongs to the People!" *(They are all laughing again.)*

ANNA.   He is such an idiot.

LUDMILLA.   But he's right, of course.

ANNA.   *Sex* belongs to the People. It's the only thing left they don't have to stand in line for.

SERGEY.   Speak for yourself.

ANNA.   You were such a rascal, Seryushka. On the tour to Spain —

SERGEY.   Now, Now ...

LUDMILLA.   Hold the edges, Anya ...

ANNA.   You and that lady poet from Seville. You told her you were a sea captain.

SERGEY.   When I was a kid, I had a rowboat. They told me she only slept with sailors, yachtsmen ... even stevedores. She had a passion for men of the sea. They called her the Harbor of Seville.

ANNA.   And you dropped anchor. A regular Don Juan.

SERGEY.   And now I'm Don Quixote.

ANNA.   *(Stroking his hair.)* No, no ... never.

LUDMILLA.   *(Patting the chaise.)* There. It's fixed. *(Pause.)* We can work now. We can rehearse.

ANNA.   *(Bitterly.)* Why?

SERGEY.   Anna ...

ANNA.   Nobody cares. You know that. Nobody cares about Chekhov. They want music, sex ... movies and rock stars. Billy Joel.

SERGEY.   We must work, my darlings. We must do our work. *(They are grouped together exactly like the three sisters at the end of that play: Anna seated, Sergey standing behind her, Ludmilla seated on the floor, leaning against the chaise.)*

ANNA.   Work. Yes ...

LUDMILLA.   But we do have to ask why, Sergey. For whom do we work? I wish I knew that. It used to be so clear.

ANNA.   It was too clear. Too simple.

SERGEY.   Nonsense. Who cares? We are artists. And now we can do whatever we like. No censorship. We can do *anything!*

ANNA.   Yes, but why?

LUDMILLA.   We used to do it for *life;* now we do it for a living. *(Pause.)*

ANNA.   I just wish I knew why. *(Slow fade to:)*

Scene 5

Stage left.

Nina posing for photos. Nina clutches a frilly dress in front of her, but is apparently nude except for high heeled shoes, white stockings and a straw sailor hat, the kind children used to wear at the turn of the century. Boris is unseen, but we hear his voice after each flash of the photo strobe. Flash.

BORIS. *(Offstage.)* Good, Nina. Very good. *(Flash.)* Smile for me ... talk to me. *(Flash.)* She pouts ... she is a naughty child ... *(Nina does so. Flash.)* It is her name day. She is so excited! *(Flash.)* Oh! Through the door comes a soldier! *(Flash.)* She is terrified! *(Flash.)* Ah, it is only the Major, after all. The Lovesick Major! *(Flash.)* She likes the Major ... *(Flash.)* She wants the Major ... *(Flash.)* But she is a good little girl, isn't she. Isn't she a good little girl, Ninchka? *(Nina turns her back, which is nude. She looks saucily over her shoulder at the "camera.")* Oh yes. She's a *good* little girl ... *(Flash. Blackout.)*

Scene 6

The Quick-Change Room.

Nikolai is in disarray, one boot on, the other off, etc. Marya is changing him, alone.

NIKOLAI. My cuffs! My cuffs!!
MARYA. I can't ...
NIKOLAI. I'm supposed to have the fancy cuffs! Where are they?!
MARYA. I couldn't find them. Lena always took care of.... It's more important you wear the right trousers. Take those off.

41

NIKOLAI. I *can't* when my boot's still on!

MARYA. Oh my god ... *(They wrestle with his boot.)*

NIKOLAI. These are too small. I've always said these are too fucking small! *(Timofey enters.)*

TIMOFEY. Nikolai, where *are* you?! You won't make your cue!

NIKOLAI. *(Pointing to Marya.)* Ask *her!*

MARYA. There! It's off. Now the trousers —

NIKOLAI. No, there's no time. Put my boots back on, you stupid cow!

TIMOFEY. *(Looking through rack.)* Where's the brown frock coat?!

MARYA. On the chair! *(She wrestles with the boot. Timofey puts coat on Nikolai.)*

NIKOLAI. I have never missed an entrance in twenty-seven years. I have never missed —

VOICE OVER P.A. SYSTEM. Nikolai Dubrovsky to stage right ... you are late! *(Nikolai hobbles off, holding one boot.)*

MARYA. *(In tears.)* ... I can't do this by myself.... Can't you see that?... It's impossible.... *(Timofey exits. Fade to:)*

Scene 7

Sergey's Office.

Timofey is following Sergey into the office.

TIMOFEY. No, no, Sergey. Please. Don't go in there!

SERGEY. My office? I can't go into my office? *(Boris enters from R. with a large bunch of office supplies: ledgers, etc., which he plunks down on Sergey's desk. He looks up in surprise to see Sergey.)*

BORIS. Ah. Sergey —

SERGEY. Don't tell me I have to wade through all that stuff? *(Laughing.)* Am I the business manager too, now?

TIMOFEY. *(To Boris.)* I was going to tell him. You said *after* four!

BORIS.   We couldn't wait. There's no room for me down there.

SERGEY.   What are you talking about?

BORIS.   My old office. You heard the announcement.

SERGEY.   You're moving in ... with me?

BORIS.   No. You see —

TIMOFEY.   *(To Sergey.)* You remember Yasha's office on the third floor? The one with the window? Right on the Fontanka? You can see the bridge, the canal ... the little boats ...

SERGEY.   I am being moved to the third floor?

BORIS.   Sergey, we must all make little sacrifices at this critical period.

SERGEY.   "Little sacrifices"? I have been in this room for twenty-five years. My life is here. I spend more time here than I do at home.

TIMOFEY.   The office on the third floor has much more light, Sergey.

SERGEY.   Then why doesn't *he* go there?

BORIS.   You see, it's like this: I have to entertain clients. I have to invite important people — hotel managers, tour guides, directors of institutes. I put together what we call "packages." I have to impress them. *(He indicates the room.)* Well.

SERGEY.   And me? I don't have to impress people?

TIMOFEY.   Sergey Tarpin does not have to impress anyone. You are a legend.

SERGEY.   And in the new order, we kick legends upstairs.

BORIS.   But, Sergey, you only have to meet with ... you know, artists. *(Pause. Sergey goes to his chair and sits.)*

SERGEY.   Here I sit. Here I shall remain.

BORIS.   Seryushka ...

SERGEY.   Do you know what the Company will think? If I move upstairs?

BORIS.   The Company is learning to accommodate itself to change.

TIMOFEY.   They have to clean their own dressing rooms now.

BORIS.   We had over one-hundred maintenance workers. I cut the staff by fifty percent. I had no choice.

SERGEY. Fine. You do all your cutting and choosing on the third floor. It has a lovely view of the Fontanka. The bridge.

TIMOFEY. The boats …

SERGEY. In 1975, Boris, I sat in this chair when the Minister of Culture came to see me. I did not go to the Ministry; the Minister came here. I was advised that if I did not stop doing controversial material — *Hamlet,* for example — if I did not cease and desist, we would no longer be allowed to operate as a State theater. In other words, we would cease to exist. I advised the Minister that she would have to deal with the thousands of Leningraders who were lining up, months in advance, to buy our tickets. I advised her that this was a temple of artistic expression for the *People.* She left. We continued. I was never harassed again. Now you, a businessman, are trying to threaten me —

BORIS. No, Sergey.

SERGEY. — are trying to threaten me and *worse,* to ease me out. First the third floor and then what? *(Pause.)* Then what?

BORIS. We don't know yet, Sergey Sergeyevich. It will depend on the productions, won't it? How well they do.

SERGEY. How good they are?

BORIS. How *well* they *do.* *(Pause.)*

SERGEY. Here I sit. Here I stay. *(Boris picks up phone.)*

BORIS. *(On phone.)* Maintenance, please … Petya?… Boris. Petya, I need a piece of furniture moved…. From the second floor to the third. Bring along three men, Petya…. A chair…. It's very heavy. There's something in it…. Just do as I say, Petya! *(He slams down receiver.)*

SERGEY. *(Imitating him, with Nazi salute.)* "Mach schnell!" *(Pause.)*

BORIS. Don't push me too far, Sergey. I can be pushed too far. *(Fade to:)*

Scene 8

The Quick-Change Room.

Music. A tour de force display of quick-change virtuosity: Nikolai, Ludmilla and Anna are changed in succession, each one a complete costume change effected by Marya.

Ludmilla goes from a courtesan to a nun.

Anna goes from a Venetian carnival masquer to a George Sand look-alike in trousers and jacket.

Nikolai goes from a serf to a bishop.

NIKOLAI.   Hat!... Hat!! *(Marya can't find his bishop's crown. Nikolai grabs a woman's hat from a hook, puts it on and exits, as Marya — having found the crown — tries to catch up with him. She collapses to the floor.)*
MARYA.   Mother of God, I need Lena! I can't do this ... I can't ... I can't do this ... *(Sob! Blackout.)*

Scene 9

Boris' Office. Formerly Sergey's.

Nina is talking with Boris.

NINA.   We just keep going over and over the same material. We're getting nowhere. It'll be like all his productions: ambiguous. Neither a happy ending nor a sad one. Just a big question mark.
BORIS.   The public doesn't pay to see question marks. That's what they deal with all day.
NINA.   Well, I just feel ... I mean, I hate to be a *noodge*,

but —

BORIS.   You have to stand up for —

NINA.   It's Ludmilla who slows everything down. Questions everything. Of course, she's a wonderful actress. We all know that. And has been. For years and years. It's just ... I don't know ...

BORIS.   Tell me what you want us to do.

NINA.   I just think ... I just think a whole new approach. A breath of fresh air. A new ...

BORIS.   Tell me what you want me to do.

NINA.   ... A new ... director, maybe. Oh, I can't believe I said that! Sergey has been like a father to me.

BORIS.   Yes, well we all have to leave our fathers sometime, don't we?

NINA.   Oh, Borya, I can see what a new *Three Sisters* — a *Three Sisters* for *today* could be! So exciting! That's what people want now, isn't it? Excitement? *(He goes to her, strokes her hair and puts his arms around her.)*

BORIS.   Tell me what you want me to do. *(Pause.)*

NINA.   Is the door closed? *(Fade to:)*

Scene 10

The Quick-Change Room.

Marya alone. Lena enters.

MARYA.   Lena!

LENA.   *(Subdued.)* Hello, Marya Stepanovna.

MARYA.   How are you? You don't look good, Lena. I was always honest with you. You look like hell.

LENA.   I manage. I'll sit down, if you don't mind, Marya.

MARYA.   Sit. Sit. I'll get you a glass of tea.

LENA.   Oh, that would be lovely. *(Marya prepares tea.)*

MARYA.   So, how's the new apartment?

LENA.   Such luxury. A big refrigerator even.

MARYA.   And Katya? Job keeping her busy?

LENA.   Oh, yes ... *(Looks around.)* Nothing's changed here.

MARYA.   Lena, you would never believe what I have to do. I *just* make the changes. *Just.* I need you.

LENA.   Do you suppose — ?

MARYA.   Never. They just keep letting people go. It's a purge! *(She closes the door.)* You come to work; there's a note in your mail slot and you're through. And where do you go? Not everyone's got a successful daughter like your Katya.

LENA.   No. *(They drink tea.)*

MARYA.   So.

LENA.   I was going to ask you ... well, first if you need any sewing or anything. Very cheap. I do that now. And then ... in the evenings, would it be all right ... just every now and then ... if I came here? Just to sit. I could help. For nothing, I mean. Just to be —

MARYA.   Lenya, what's wrong?

LENA.   ... just to have somewhere to go.

MARYA.   What's wrong with your apartment? *(Nina bustles in, dressed to the nines.)*

NINA.   Lena! What a surprise. How are you?

LENA.   Hello, Nina. *(They embrace.)* My! Quite the lady!

MARYA.   She buys all these fancy clothes ...

NINA.   No concern of yours. *(She goes behind dressing screen and changes into rehearsal clothes during the following.)*

MARYA.   You see? My daughter, the big star. Hasn't even opened yet and already she's a big star.

LENA.   Well, it's wonderful, how they do.

MARYA.   They do?

LENA.   How they get on. The young ones.

MARYA.   I'll tell you how that one gets on.

NINA.   Mother ...

MARYA.   She gets on Boris and rides him to the bank.

NINA.   Buzz, buzz, buzz. Listen to the gossip around here.

MARYA.   She has no shame. None at all.

NINA.   You know nothing about it.

MARYA.   Yes, well, I wish you had an honest job like Lena's Katya. Working as a hostess. Working with respectable people —

NINA. Katya's a prostitute. *(Pause.)* Didn't you know that, mother?

MARYA. *(Whispered.)* Lena ... *(Nina comes from behind the screen.)*

NINA. Didn't you know that? She's a hooker.

LENA. *(Standing.)* And what are *you*?

NINA. I hear she won't let you stay in the apartment while she's "working." Well, who would want to: all that moaning and groaning —

LENA. *(Starting out.)* I'm going.

MARYA. Shut up, Nina! Lena, oh my god ... oh, my poor little Lenya. It's true, then? *(She hugs Lena. They are both crying.)*

NINA. Look, I'm sorry, but you started it with all those insinuations. *(No reply.)* I'm off. Rehearsal. You should come by more often, Lena. Mama needs someone to talk to. "Hi" to Katya. *(She leaves.)*

MARYA. They can't wait, you see? They've got to have it all right now. We came from a different world. We were happy just to work.

LENA. I must go. If Boris were to find me here —

MARYA. Let him. This is my domain!

LENA. Be careful, Marya. I'll go home. Katya doesn't usually have ... clients until the evening. She goes to the American bar at the Evropeskaya or the Astoria ... then they come back. I go to the films, but they're so expensive now ...

MARYA. You come here. Anytime.

LENA. Thank you, Marya. *(She goes to the door. Stops. Turns back.)* I don't understand what we were doing that was wrong. Why it all had to be changed ... *(Lights fade.)*

Scene 11

The Rehearsal Room

Ludmilla, Anna and Nina are rehearsing the final scene. Timofey holds book; Sergey watches. Far upstage, Nikolai is sitting listening to a Walkman with a headset.

NINA. "Someday it will all be perfectly clear. Why all this suffering.... Someday.... But for now, we must simply get on with it. Work. It's almost winter. Soon, there'll be snow, snow over everything. But I don't care. I will work ... just *work.*"

LUDMILLA. "And the days will pass, and we will pass with them.... Gone. Forgotten. What we looked like ... the sound of our voices ... all, all forgotten. They won't remember who we were, how many of us there were. But what we are going through — all this pain — it will allow things to change. For those who come after.... Peace ... happiness. For them. O, my sisters ... O my sisters, life isn't over yet! We *live.* Just a while longer and then we'll know. What it all meant. Why we suffered so much.... If only we knew.... If only we knew ..." *(Pause.)*

SERGEY. But I think ... I think, Nina darling, it is not yet *in* you. In ... as Konstantin Sergeyevich used to say ... "in the bone." *(He turns away.)*

NINA. *(Whispered, to Anna.)* "Konstantin Sergeyevich?"

ANNA and LUDMILLA. Stanislavsky!

SERGEY. *(Turning back.)* What?

TIMOFEY. Nothing, Sergey.

SERGEY. You speak the words beautifully, Nina my angel. But they come from your lips. Ludmilla also speaks beautifully, but her words come from the *bone.* She is *there.* The suffering which she refers to ... it is simply *there.* How is this achieved?

LUDMILLA. *(Ruefully.)* I could tell you.

SERGEY. Hmm?

NINA. It is true, Sergey, Ludmilla has known the world far, far longer than I have. But you know, perhaps Irina ... is not *there* yet. I don't mean me, Nina. I mean Irina.

LUDMILLA. But the Baron has just been killed!

NINA. She doesn't give a damn about the Baron.

LUDMILLA. Oh, surely —

NINA. She doesn't give a damn about anyone. "I have never known what love is," she says. She realizes — as so few women did ... do — that she is *on her own.* No one will do anything for her.

SERGEY. There! That was *there!* You were there.

LUDMILLA. Yes, but now she must do that with Chekhov's words.

NINA. Maybe if I could use my own words —

LUDMILLA. You will use the playwright's words! That is what we do here. It is called Art.

NINA. I am aware of that, Ludi.

LUDMILLA. "Ludi!?"

ANNA. Tea time, everyone. Time for tea.

TIMOFEY. I have it ready. In the salon.

SERGEY. Fifteen minutes, my angels. Where is my water? *(He searches, as Nina, Ludmilla and Timofey exit.)*

ANNA. Here it is, Seryushka.

SERGEY. I used to run rehearsals; now they run me.

ANNA. You know what I think, Sergey?

SERGEY. Don't you want your tea?

ANNA. I think we have rehearsed enough.

SERGEY. It's not there yet.

ANNA. If we don't open something, *soon,* the theater won't be "there." We keep dropping plays from the repertory, but nothing new opens. And you know Gubin has opened *Lolita* at the Maly and it is a great hit.

SERGEY. Don't mention that charlatan's name.

ANNA. We have to compete, Sergey! Though whether Chekhov will compete with Nabokov ... I don't know.

SERGEY. Chekhov will always compete. Chekhov is king. *(Boris enters, followed by Timofey.)*

BORIS. Sergey Sergeyevich?

SERGEY. Yes?

BORIS. If you could be so kind ... Timofey has brought you your tea. May I have a word?

TIMOFEY. Here is your tea, Sergey.

SERGEY. And for Anna? Where is hers?

ANNA. I'll go, Sergey. Boris and you should talk. *(She leaves them.)*

BORIS. *(Bowing.)* Anna.

TIMOFEY. *(Bowing.)* Anna. *(Anna exits.)*

BORIS. A goddess, that one.

SERGEY. What do you want, Boris? Are you moving me out

to the courtyard?

BORIS.   Sergey, you know perfectly well your new office suits you. And you have fewer idiots coming in to bother you up there. You have time to think.

TIMOFEY.   To look out your window.

SERGEY.   Get to the point.

BORIS.   I have been meeting with the Marketing Committee —

SERGEY.   Imagine! A theater with a "Marketing Committee."

BORIS.   The days of self-indulgence are over. We have to show the public what they *want* to see.

SERGEY.   How do *they* know?! We have to show it to them first.

BORIS.   I'm not going to discuss theory with you. Here's what we want to do: We're not going to scrap *The Three Sisters*. But we can't possibly sell yet another traditional production. So ... we want, so to speak ... an adaptation. A new look at *The Three Sisters*.

SERGEY.   Of course a new look. That is what —

BORIS.   — with music.

SERGEY.   Ivan is composing a score, as always.

BORIS.   No, no. With *music*, Sergey. Songs.... Maybe some dances. *(Pause.)* A musical. *(Pause.)*

SERGEY.   A musical? A musical comedy? Of *The Three Sisters?!*

BORIS.   That's it.

TIMOFEY.   It will be fun!

SERGEY.   Fun?

TIMOFEY.   Oh yes, Sergey.

SERGEY.   Timofey, I strongly suggest you get behind some large piece of furniture.

TIMOFEY.   Sergey?

SERGEY.   Because I am going to injure you.

BORIS.   Now, now, Sergey. Let's be civilized.

SERGEY.   You suggest turning *The Three Sisters* into a musical and you suggest we be civilized? At the same time?

BORIS.   Here is the script. *(Timofey gingerly hands a large manuscript to Sergey.)* As you will see, a score has been written. Pavel Turnish has written the songs —

SERGEY. Pavel Turnish? Who is —

BORIS. There are some significant changes, of course. For instance, the sisters *do* get to Moscow.

SERGEY. *(Leafing through script.)* This is ... garbage ... rubbish.... What's this?

> "Meet me in Moscow
> And won't it be grand
> We'll kiss by the Kremlin
> And I'll hold your hand" ...?!

Or this:

> "Stay with me, Masha, and don't ever part,
> The town is on fire and so is my heart"!!

(He throws script on floor.) Never! And you won't get the actors to take part in this drivel, either. *(Since the arrival of Boris, Nikolai has taken off his headset, and has been eavesdropping. Now he comes D.)*

NIKOLAI. Actually, Sergey, some of us are rather keen to try it. I myself am studying singing. *(He holds out his Walkman.)* From an instructional tape my brother got in Berlin. I think all my life I have secretly been ... a tenor.

SERGEY. Your secret is safe with me. *(Nina enters, followed by Anna and Ludmilla. They have been listening at the door.)*

NINA. I want to do this, too. I've always felt Irina should sing ... should dance. Since that first day of rehearsal, Sergey, when we danced. I have trouble just speaking the lines. I want to take off!

SERGEY. Anna! Ludmilla. Surely you would never stoop to this sort of cheap theatricality?

ANNA. It is for you to decide, Sergey. You are our leader. *(To Boris.)* Don't forget that.

SERGEY. Ludi?

LUDMILLA. Sergey ... *(She comes to him.)* Sergey Sergeyevich ... I can't sing. I have never been able to. The whole thing is quite impossible.

BORIS. Well, in fact, Sergey, if you look through this new version you will see ... there are only two sisters. Not three.

SERGEY. What?!

BORIS. We ... that is to say, the Committee felt that the

character of Olga is really antitheatrical. I mean what does she do, really, except bitch and moan? Both Masha and Irina have love stories. Olga just stands behind the dressing screen and watches, doesn't she? *(Ludmilla falls to her knees before Sergey.)*

LUDMILLA.   Save me, Sergey! Save me from this!

SERGEY.   Olga has the great, final speech. Olga has the beautiful opening speech. Olga is the *glue* which holds the Prozorov family together.

BORIS.   "Glue," yes. An apt description.

LUDMILLA.   Sergey ... *please* ...

SERGEY.   Get up, my angel. Get up. *(She does.)* Ludmilla and I refuse to have anything to do with this harebrained scheme. And Anna, of course, agrees. Call the others.

BORIS.   The others have already received their scripts and are ... making the necessary adjustments.

SERGEY.   I am cancelling this production!

BORIS.   No, you are not. And any company member who refuses to participate ... or who cannot participate ... will be dismissed. *(Pause.)* That includes, of course, the director. *(Sergey looks to Anna.)*

ANNA.   I have to work, Sergey. I have no choice. *(Sergey walks to the chaise longue and touches it tenderly. He turns to the others and declaims dramatically.)*

SERGEY.   Treason! Treason in the highest degree!!

BORIS.   This is not a kingdom, Sergey. This is a business.

SERGEY.   Business! *(He sits on chaise. Ludmilla rushes to sit by his side.)*

BORIS.   We have asked Timofey to take over rehearsals, anticipating your ... behavior.

ANNA.   Sergey, don't refuse. *Please.* Don't turn the company over to this imbecile. *(Points to Timofey.)*

SERGEY.   Company? What Company? It is no longer a company. It is a group of employees.

BORIS.   Semantics. And grand sentimentality, Sergey. In point of fact, I am saving the Company. Our box office has dropped to nothing. People who can still afford to go the theater are flocking to see *Lolita* at the Maly. Or they go to the opera, the ballet. Now we will show them something brand new. Full of color and life! The new Kuzlov. The new star of St. Petersburg! I am saving you all. Saving you! *(He goes up and sits by Sergey.)* I could go into the restaurant business, Sergey, like all my friends. Make a killing. I have a family to support. I finally got my kid into a clinic. In Munich. Will it work? I don't know, but we try. And you, Sergey Sergeyevich, you want to make me feel guilty? "Treason"! Forget it. Have you read *The Three Sisters*, Sergey? "Life goes on. We must work."

SERGEY. The Devil can cite Chekhov for his purpose. I will not work with the Devil.

LUDMILLA. And what about me? Thirty years I have worked — worked *hard*. For thirty years. *(Points to Nina.)* Before this one was born. Haven't I earned the right to be respected here? *(To Anna.)* Haven't I?

ANNA. Of course, Ludi. Of course.

BORIS. Don't worry, Ludi old pet. We'll find something for you to do. *(He gets up and starts out.)* You make up your mind, Sergey. And let me know. Rehearsals start tomorrow. *(He exits. Timofey picks up the script and starts out, followed by Nikolai.)*

NIKOLAI. I have an idea, Timofey: When Vershinin and Masha come in from the snow ... a sleighing song, don't you think?... "Ho Ho Ho, Look at all the snow" ... sort of thing. What do you think? *(They exit.)*

NINA. You all think I'm terrible. I know. I even understand. But the thing we all have to do now — and without rules or regulations, or guarantees from anyone ... the thing we all have to do now ... is survive. *(She leaves slowly. Anna and Ludmilla are seated on the chaise with Sergey.)*

ANNA. So.

LUDMILLA. So. Just two sisters now. That is what our great Russian theater has come down to: *The Two Sisters* ... by Anton Pavlovich ... Chekhov. *(Lights fade.)*

Scene 12

Boris' Office.

Boris on phone.

BORIS.   You will *love* it, Alicia my angel. And your tourist groups will love it, too ... no, no, no, Chekhov is not always Chekhov. You come by the theater tomorrow morning and look at the posters out front. You will be amazed.... No, we're not using that title anymore ... *(Timofey enters holding a poster which he unrolls and shows to Boris.)* Now it's called: *O My Sister! (And we see the sexy photo of Nina with the title,* O My Sister! *printed diagonally over her bare bottom. Blackout.)*

Scene 13

The Quick-Change Room.

Marya and Lena sewing.

Sasha enters. He wears a sharp Armani suit. His hair has been moussed and he has a fashionable one-day's growth of beard on his face.

MARYA.   Sasha!
SASHA.   Where is he? I'll kill him!
LENA.   Who?
SASHA.   Boris.
MARYA.   It's a very good idea, Sasha, but no. Don't do anything crazy. Look at you! *(Patting his suit.)* All this in the provinces?
SASHA.   That's where the action is.
LENA.   My goodness ...
SASHA.   I ran into a few of my old buddies. One thing led

to another. We run a little ... import-export business. The only one in town. And we make damn sure it stays that way. Where's Nina?

MARYA. Big rehearsal today, Sasha. Big changes.

SASHA. Is it true? What I hear?

MARYA. She's going to be a star now, Sasha. You'll be very proud of her.

SASHA. I've seen the "star" out on the billboard. Naked as the day she was born.

LENA. She's wearing a hat.

SASHA. I'm gonna take her away from all this. Boris is treating her like a *whore.*

MARYA. Calm down, Sasha. Calm down!

SASHA. Yeah ... well.... So. How's everything with you two? How's your Katya? *(Lena bursts into tears and goes behind the screen.)* What'd I say? *(Nina enters.)*

NINA. Sasha!

SASHA. Good. You've got some clothes on.

NINA. Sasha ... my god, look at you! Sasha ... you're magnificent!

SASHA. I've come to kill Boris.

NINA. Now, Sasha. There's really no need. Boris is my ... my mentor.

SASHA. "Helping your career?"

NINA. Exactly.

SASHA. With payments made in bed!

NINA. *(Slaps him.)* How dare you!

MARYA. I'll just leave you two. I'll just go visit Lena. *(She goes behind screen.)*

NINA. In the first place, what I do is my business. In the second place, may I remind you that you left St. Petersburg and haven't written in months. And in the third place, it's not true!

SASHA. That's not what I hear.

NINA. Boris likes to brag. With the boys. I flirt with him. That's all.

SASHA. That's terrible. Flirting with married men.

NINA. Look, we do what we have to.

56

MARYA. *(From behind screen.)* I'm hearing all this. I hear every word ...

SASHA. If I see Boris, I'll kill him. *(He pulls out a gun. Lena and Marya scream behind the dressing screen.)*

NINA. Oooh! A real gun. I guess you've gone into another line of work.

SASHA. I'm in the import-export business. We get things for people. That they need.

NINA. Sort of like Boris. Well, Sasha, whatever works, you know? But you really don't need to kill Boris. He could be a big customer for you.

SASHA. I wouldn't dirty my hands.

NINA. I think you might, Sashenka. Mother, I need my third-act dress. Is it done?

MARYA. *(From screen.)* On the chair.

NINA. They want me to try this in the dance number. Pretty, isn't it? *(She pats Sasha's hair.)* What a man you are now, Sasha. Come up to my dressing room. I've got a big one all to myself. You can help me ... change.

SASHA. I don't know ...

NINA. I love that gun, Sasha. Come on. We haven't got all day.

SASHA. All right ... *(As they leave.)* But if I see Boris ...

NINA. Boom-boom. *(We hear her laughter trailing away. Pause.)*

MARYA. *(From behind screen.)* Were we ever like that, Lena?

LENA. *(Behind screen.)* I don't think so.... *(Pause.)* No. *(Lights fade.)*

Scene 14

Boris' Office.

Boris and Timofey in evening clothes.

TIMOFEY. It is a great turn-out, Boris. Even the American consul, and he never goes to cultural affairs.

BORIS. The Kuzlov Theater is back on top! Where's Sergey?

TIMOFEY. He's in his office on the third floor, Boris. He won't come down. He just sits there. Looking out the window.

BORIS. Feeling sorry for himself.

TIMOFEY. He was a great man, Boris.

BORIS. *(Angry.)* I know that! You think I don't know that?! *(Calmer.)* We don't need great men now. We need clever men. Then, after a time, the great men can come back downstairs. People like you and me have to do the dirty work. I resigned myself to that years ago.

TIMOFEY. Nothing to be ashamed of.

BORIS. Oh, I'm not. Not at all! Look, Timofey. *(He produces a bottle of champagne.)* French champagne!

TIMOFEY. Must've cost a fortune!

BORIS. Sasha got it for me. We'll drink it later. To our success.

TIMOFEY. To *O My Sister! (Music heard.)* It's time! *(Blackout.)*

Scene 15

The Quick-Change Room.

Marya and Lena are sewing.

MARYA. It will start soon.

LENA. So many quick-changes.

MARYA. It's a musical.

LENA. What I don't understand…. Why did they fire me, and then give Ludmilla my old job?

MARYA. Boris said: "Loyalty is important." He wasn't going to put Ludi out on the streets, was he? After thirty years in the Company?

LUDMILLA. *(Entering dressed as a wardrobe mistress.)* So degrading.

MARYA. Now, now.

LENA. Consider yourself fortunate, Ludi. At least you've got a job.

MARYA. And there's an art to it. You'll see. Lena will teach you.

LUDMILLA. For a fee!

LENA. It's only fair. You've got a job; I don't.

LUDMILLA. Imagine. Not having a job. That used to be illegal.

MARYA. Yes, well ... now we have freedom. *(Long pause. They all laugh.)* I wouldn't mind all this ... all this hardship, if we knew when it would end. When there's a war, you know it'll end. One way or the other. When you're sick, it has to end. Labor pains end. But this is different. *(Pause.)* If only we knew.

LUDMILLA. Yes. If only we knew ... *(They sit there, sewing, as the Quick-Change Room wagons U. A set piece flies in to tell us we are now onstage. Nina walks into a spotlight. Anna stands U. of her. They are in costume for the final scene of* O My Sister!*)*

Scene 16

The Finale.

NINA. *(As Irina.)* "No, Masha. I'm not going to wait any longer. The soldiers are leaving. And I'm leaving, too! I can't stay here another minute. After all, why should I?" *(Sings.)*
> Good-bye old life!
> Hello new life!
> Moscow, here I come!
>
> I'm gonna climb aboard
> That Moscow train.
> I'm gonna pack my bags
> And say good-bye
> To all that pain.
> I'm gonna laugh and never look back,
> I'm gonna smile every mile
> Of that clickety-clack!
> So clear the track!

I'm gonna change my life
On the Moscow train!
Don't try to stop me now
'Cause if you do
You'll try in vain!
I'll say good-bye to all of these jerks.
I'm gonna pay my own way
Gonna shoot the works!
I'll shoot the works!

Hear that whistle
Blowin' round the bend?
Come on, Masha,
To the Happy End!

(Nikolai, as Vershinin, comes running on in his greatcoat and military hat. He holds a valise.)

NIKOLAI. "I've changed my mind! I can't leave you. I can't get on that train!"

ANNA. *(As Masha.)* "Oh, yes you can!"

NINA. "Masha!"

ANNA. "'Cause I'm leaving *with* you!"

NINA and NIKOLAI. "Hooray!"

NINA. *(Singing.)*
Here it comes!

ANNA and NIKOLAI. *(Singing.)*
Yes, yes, yes!

NIKOLAI.
Hop on board!

ALL THREE.
The Moscow Express!

NINA and ANNA.
We can wear our finest finery
Dining in that elegant dinery.

NIKOLAI.
The caviar and blintzes you chew
Eating on that Moscow choo-choo
You can charge to me:
I'm a Colonel — I ride for free!!

NINA and ANNA.

     He's a colonel he rides for free!!

ALL THREE.

     We're gonna climb aboard

     That Moscow train!

     We're gonna change our life

NIKOLAI.

     (And leave my wife.)

ALL THREE.

     And not complain.

     We're gonna leave the sorrow and strife!

ANNA.

     Gonna clear out of here!

NIKOLAI.

     Gonna race from this place!

NINA.

     Gonna jump from this dump!

ALL THREE.

     Gonna fly from this sty!

     To a brand, new, *life!!* YES!!

(A cut-out of a steam engine rolls in, with much smoke and bell ring-ing. Nina, Anna and Nikolai hop on board and are carried offstage. Far U.C. we see Marya, Lena and Ludmilla in the Quick-Change Room. The three ladies sit there, quietly sewing, as the curtain falls.)

THE END

PROPERTY LIST

Cigarette (SERGEY)
Stopwatch (TIMOFEY)
Elegant wooden pipe, trousers, hat, epaulets,
    sword belt (MARYA, LENA, NIKOLAI)
Skirt (MARYA)
Jacket (LENA)
New clothing (MARYA, LENA)
Change chart (MARYA)
Telephone (BORIS)
Stage light (SASHA, TIMOFEY)
Play script (TIMOFEY)
Notebook (BORIS)
Armor pieces (NIKOLAI)
Costume for Nikolai (MARYA, LENA)
Wig, coat, trousers (MARYA, LENA)
Valise (SASHA)
Bag of instant coffee (BORIS)
Package of rose water (MARYA)
Costume hat (NIKOLAI)
Hat, cloak, gloves for Anna (MARYA, LENA)
Dress (NINA)
Monk's clothing (NIKOLAI)
Hat (MARYA)
Robe (MARYA)
Sewing paraphernalia (LUDMILLA, MARYA, LENA)
Frilly dress (NINA)
Boot (MARYA, NIKOLAI)
Office supplies (BORIS)
Bishop's crown (MARYA)
Woman's hat (NIKOLAI)
Tea (MARYA)

Rehearsal clothes (NINA)
Walkman (NIKOLAI)
Glass of tea (TIMOFEY)
Poster (TIMOFEY)
Gun (SASHA)
Champagne (BORIS)
Valise (NIKOLAI)

SOUND EFFECTS

Roars of audience laughter
Electric warning bell
Applause
Train bell

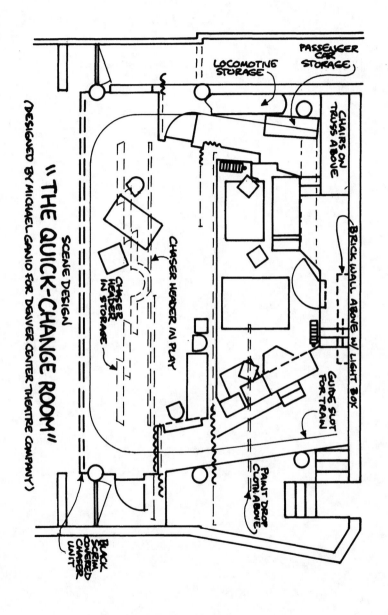

SCENE DESIGN
"THE QUICK-CHANGE ROOM"
(DESIGNED BY MICHAEL GANIO FOR DENVER CENTER THEATRE COMPANY)

LOCOMOTIVE STORAGE

PASSENGER CAR STORAGE

CHAIRS ON TRUSS ABOVE

BRICK WALL ABOVE W/ LIGHT BOX

CHASER HEADER IN PLAY

CHASER HEADER IN STORAGE

GUIDE SLOT FOR TRAIN

PAINT DROP CLOTH ABOVE

BLACK SCRIM COVERED CHASER UNIT